Brian's Thought's

Brian Shaun Watson

Contents

Yearning for a Voice...1

Nat's Everywhere 2

Fighting Hate 3

The 1980's...4

A Time of Great Change..5

A Great Day For A Walk!...6

The Smartphone Addiction...7

The Sweet Cherry Blossom's 8

Tom Hank's Interview..9

The Purpose of Democrats..10

The Magic of Romantic Love..11

Fear of the Dentist...12

Extreme Rage...13

Rage In His Eyes..14

A Beautiful Starry Night..15

The beauty of falling rain on a cloudy day 16

The Prettiest Girl I Have Ever Seen......................................17

The Woman Holding an Umbrella..18

Feeling Great..19

A Typical Day At Work..20

What Do We Fear? 21

Voices In My Head...22

Wishing I Was Rich..23

Yearning for A Better World to Live In 24

About The Author..25

Yearning for a Voice

Sitting at home wondering what it all means and just wishing I had a voice in the world like some of these famous 80's singers like Tina Turner and George Michael. You know just simply wanting to be heard and have an effect on social change in the world at large through my poetry. That's all.

Nat's Everywhere

Nat's here, Nat's there, Nat's everywhere.

Fighting Hate

I really think it's sad to see what's happening to the transgender community right now here in the United States of America. Actually, it's just not right the way I see it. I mean what gives somebody the right in this country or any country for that matter the right to take a group like the transgender community's rights simply because somebody is afraid of something they don't or want to understand like the Republican party is doing right now across the country. I mean it's just plain not right. I mean everybody in any society should have the right to be free from hatred and bigotry especially here in the good old US of A. Because If they are not free from that bigotry and hatred. Then everything this country is supposed to stand for which is "Life, Liberty, and The pursuit of happiness has no meaning anymore. Especially in a so-called Democracy like the United States of America.

The 1980's

I was just thinking about at work today how much I miss the 1980s. I mean I don't care what anybody says. That was definitely the best decade ever of the 20th century for art, pop culture, and the music industry. That's for sure! I mean I don't know how many times I watched the movie Flashdance, and Empire Strikes Back during that decade. Especially the movie Flashdance! I mean I really loved that movie to death! I also loved the movie Empire Strikes Back! I definitely couldn't get enough of that movie and of course, the carbon freeze scene was always my fave! Another good movie I really liked during the 1980s was the ever enthralling inception meet's Freddy Krueger type of premise "Dream Scape." You know the movie that talked about inception type of themes years before Inception ever hit theatres. I mean what a decade to be alive especially a child like I was during the 1980s. I mean I have to admit that the best time of my life was growing up in an exciting time like the 1980s. That's For Sure!

A Time of Great Change

It's just hard to believe all of the rapid changes that are happening in the world right now. Political or otherwise. I mean it's just absolutely amazing! It's a great time in World History to be alive right now I think. Personally speaking from my perspective.

A Great Day For A Walk!

What a wonderfully perfect day for going for a walk today here
in good old Nashville, Tennessee. I mean the sun was shining.
Not a cloud in the sky. Just a perfect day for a nice walk around
the good old neighborhood. That's for Damn Sure!

The Smartphone Addiction

You know the one thing I could never understand is the
millennial's addiction to their phones. I mean I get bored after
about a few minutes of looking at my smartphone. I guess I
would have to be a millennial and a computer geek like my
brother and my father to understand. That's at least the only thing
that would make any logical sense Right?

The Sweet Cherry Blossom's

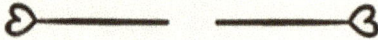

I was taking a walk around my neighborhood this morning and thinking about how pretty the newly blossomed sweet cherry tree blossoms were on the trees that surrounded my apartment complex here at Hillmont Condominiums.

Tom Hank's Interview

I was just watching an interview with the now-famous actor Tom Hank's on the 60 Minutes Australia on the YouTube channel and I learned some stuff about him I didn't like. For example, he buys and collects old vintage typewriters. Kind of cool uh?

The Purpose of Democrats

What does it mean to be a progressive? Well, what I think it means is standing up for the little guy or standing up for people who can't otherwise stand up or speak up for themselves. I mean what's the purpose of being a progressive if you don't do these things I just mentioned, you know? I mean the whole purpose of being someone who claims to be a Democrat or Progressive is the strong standing up for the weak. That's all I'm saying.

The Magic of Romantic Love

I was watching the movie Tributes to the 1980s on the YouTube channel and got me thinking about it like I always do when I watch the tribute to the power and magic of never-ending romantic love.

Fear of the Dentist

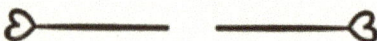

There's nothing that I fear more than going to the dentist. Because I'm always afraid of getting my tooth drilled for one reason or another. I can tell you there is no pain worse than getting one of your teeth drilled on by the dentist. The only thing worse than getting your teeth drilled on by the dentist is getting one of your teeth pulled! Trust me, I know! I mean I had that done to me not too long ago and I have to tell you it's the worst, most unbearable pain I have ever felt in my entire life! I mean I don't care what anybody else says there's no way you can't be in pain the whole time the Dentist is trying to take one of your teeth out. Please take my word for it. It definitely hurts!

Extreme Rage

So much anger, So much rage.

Rage In His Eyes

Rage in his Eyes, anger in his demeanor.

A Beautiful Starry Night

Beautiful stars scattered about the beautiful night sky and a half-crescent moon shines brightly in the middle of it all.

The beauty of falling rain on a cloudy day

The sound of water falling from the heavens, the sound of water droplets hitting the pavement,

The smell of rainwater on concrete.

The Prettiest Girl I Have Ever Seen

There was this girl,

Her name was Mandy,

She had the prettiest hair I have ever seen,

She was tall and to this day I still think about her.

When I think about Mandy Miller, I wonder what could have been.

The Woman Holding an Umbrella

There a woman stands,

In The Garden,

Holding an umbrella,

Over her head,

Surrounded by colorful flowers,

And a little cute dog.

Feeling Great

Got up this morning,

Ate my cereal,

Turned on my Roku,

And I just realized how nice and rested I feel,

I also decided to catch up on some of my television shows on the
CW APP on my Roku TV.

A Typical Day At Work

My job at Vanderbilt has gotten pretty dull and repetitive. I mean it feels kind of weird, like I'm in the Twilight Zone or something. Especially, when I greet people on my way to work even though it's the same people I see every day. You know like something out of a movie or something. Like something of a dream or something. That's all.

What Do We Fear?

What do we fear as human beings? When it ultimately comes down to it? Change, An uncertain future, the unknown? That's a good question. Whatever it is we need to figure out right now in this day and time if we want to live in a diverse and just world. Not just for us, but for future generations to come.

Voices In My Head

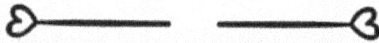

I got out of bed with voices in my head.

Wishing I Was Rich

Living from paycheck to paycheck is really hard especially when you live in an expensive city like Nashville, Tennessee. I mean, sometimes, I wish I was born into a rich family so I wouldn't have to worry about paying for the basics like food, water, and shelter. That would definitely be Nice, you know? Without a doubt.

Yearning for A Better World to Live In

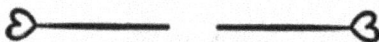

Yearning for world peace, Yearning for an end to war, Yearning for an end to sadness, Yearning for an end to hate.

About The Author

Brian Shaun Watson is an accomplished poet, showcasing a passion for the written word that dates back to his formative years in the 5th grade. Despite facing early challenges that led to the need to redo the 1st grade, Brian's tenacity and innate love for language propelled him to excel in reading and writing later in life.

Born on Friday, August 11th, 1978, in Hampton, Virginia, Brian's childhood was marked by a joyful disposition and an early affinity for music. His responsiveness to external stimuli hinted at a sensitivity that would later find expression in his poetic works.

In a parallel with the renowned poet Emily Dickinson, Brian confronted epilepsy in his early years. Additionally, he shares a diagnosis of schizoaffective disorder, a facet of his life that he openly acknowledges and uses as a source of inspiration for his creative endeavors.

Beyond his literary pursuits, Brian navigates life with resilience despite contending with an array of chronic health challenges, including allergies and chronic rhinitis. His ability to channel personal experiences into the realm of poetry reflects not only his artistic skill but also his profound understanding of the human condition.

Brian Shaun Watson's work is a testament to his journey, marked by resilience, creativity, and an unwavering dedication to the craft of poetry.

www.ingramcontent.com/pod-product-compliance
Lightning Source LLC
LaVergne TN
LVHW011339080426
835513LV00006B/440